both Christian and Jewish circles,
he has lectured in comparative
religion, conducted retreats and
been the convenor of an ecclesi-
astical court. He is also a popular
and acclaimed broadcaster, jour-
nalist, cook and author.

THE LITTLE BOOK OF
BLUE THOUGHTS

Rabbi Lionel Blue

RIDER

LONDON · SYDNEY · AUCKLAND · JOHANNESBURG

1 3 5 7 9 10 8 6 4 2

First published in 2001 by Rider, an imprint of Ebury Press,
Random House, 20 Vauxhall Bridge Road, London SW1V 2SA

Random House Australia (Pty) Limited
20 Alfred Street, Milsons Point, Sydney, New South Wales 2061,
Australia

Random House New Zealand Limited
18 Poland Road, Glenfield, Auckland 10, New Zealand

Random House South Africa (Pty) Limited
Endulini, 5A Jubilee Road, Parktown 2193, South Africa

The Random House Group Limited Reg. No. 954009
Papers used by Rider are natural, recyclable products made from
wood grown in sustainable forests.

Printed and bound in Denmark by Nørhaven A/S, Viborg

A CIP catalogue record for this book is available from the British
Library

ISBN 0-7126-1212-2

INTRODUCTION

To Life!

My greatest spiritual teacher has been Life itself. Not exotic life in a monastery high up in the Himalayas but ordinary life in London today.

Some of life's lessons have been painful and some so natural that I didn't realise at first how super-natural they were.

I have pondered on life's lessons on the tops of buses, in railway stations, at parties and when sitting silently in empty chapels, churches and synagogues.

And in the silence I have become aware of a life beyond, pulsating beneath the surface of this one.

May this book encourage you to ponder on your own life experience and to hear the Voice that speaks in it.

Le Chaim!

To Life!

God bless you!

LIONEL BLUE

Happiness

Some tips about happiness:

It's not like a quiche, when the more slices you give away the less you have for yourself. It's the opposite. The more happiness you give to others the more you'll have for yourself.

If you run after happiness, it runs after you and you never

meet. But if you forget it, it just happens.

Happiness isn't things outside you; it's a feeling, a state of mind inside you. I've been both happy and unhappy in comfortless hostels and luxury hotels. I'd sooner be unhappy in a luxury hotel, but that's not the point, is it?

Enlightenment at a Bridge Game

A young man was making a grand slam in bridge against an older couple. But instead of congratulating him, his wife mouthed, 'Fool!' – leaving him feeling hurt and bewildered. Light dawned! The older man was the young man's boss and every win in the two-dimensional world of cards was a loss in the three-dimensional world of the boss's favour.

Just as the real world encloses the world of cards, so a spiritual world encloses the real world. And a worldly gain in this life could be a loss in eternal life. So watch out!

On Offer

I used to treat God as a heavenly department store, a Harrods-on-high without price labels. I didn't ask for much, just comfort, security, health, happiness and such. But if you look at a crucifix or read up on tragic Jewish history, you realise such rewards are chancy. The time-tested reward of prayer is the growth of love that God inspires in us. That's what's on offer.

Is that all?

Probably.

Sorry!

In the Supermarket

A lady on a park bench told me how she'd nearly lost her temper in a supermarket. The woman in front of her had muddled up her credit cards and was holding up the entire queue, the checkout girl was hysterical and the frustrated man behind her was ramming her in the backside with his trolley.

'I was about to explode too,' she said, 'when I suddenly burst out laughing. I sorted the credit cards, pacified the checkout girl and even wiggled my bum to make a better target for the trolley. I don't know what came over me!'

'You had a moment of grace,' I replied. 'Lots of us have them but usually we throw them away.'

The Empty Church

Is there anything in religion for you? You'll have to provide your own answer.

Sit in an empty place of worship and let whatever happens happen. You'll need ten minutes because you'll go through layers of anxiety – 'Have I left the gas on?' Or embarrassing thoughts.

Or feeling sorry for yourself. You might cry. Or feel what nonsense it all is. But at the end there is a moment of quiet.

Do this about ten times. Something may speak to you in the quiet.

Life

'What's life?' I asked as a child. Some said the purpose of life was happiness. But happiness is far too chancy. Some said life was a school where you learnt to acquire things, and then give them back. This made sense.

I just want to add that life is like a mirror. If you look into the mirror of life with hate, it reflects it back. If you look into it with trust, it justifies some of it. So it's over to you!

Parting

I knew from something my partner said that we were breaking up after many years together. We had grown out of each other.

I sat in a chapel nearby and looked into the black hole that had opened up in my life. An inner voice then said, 'In this world you only enjoy reflections of love. But one day you will meet the real thing.'

I took this to mean that I would meet up with the inner voice that had been talking to me for so many years and that this meeting would take place at death.

Death has not worried me since then. Pain – yes, but death – no.

Status

My big black dog would only eat
her dog food if some human food
were added. Gradually, she began
to push her bowl nearer and
nearer the dining-room table,
until one day when I came back
from a business trip, after
entrusting the house to two dog-
loving friends.

My dog was now sitting at the
dining-room table, and when I

sent her sharply back to her bowl in the kitchen, she growled at me.

I sympathised with her. She was trying to improve herself and become human, though she had no idea of what being human involved.

Just as I want to improve myself and become spiritual, though I have little idea of the demands and responsibilities it brings.

The Messiah

'If they tell you the Messiah is coming just as you're planting a tree,' said the sage, 'first finish planting it and only then go out to welcome him.'

Failures

When I was a television cook everything went wrong and I was about to give up when a widower wrote to me that after his wife died, he had tried to cook for himself. He was so bad at it he ordered 'meals-on-wheels' instead, but having seen my efforts he would try again.

God works through our failures as well as our successes.

Worried –
Letter Following

We worry more now because we've got more to worry about. In childhood many of us didn't walk on the cracks between paving stones or touch things. It was our childhood insecurity. Sometimes these habits have carried on into our adult life. I wouldn't worry about them unless they are socially embarrassing. Remember, they are not about your life as it is now, but

about your insecurities long ago
– and you're in good company:
there are lots of us like you.

But there's no need to spread
anxiety. If you're on holiday,
don't send a telegram back home
saying, 'It's all so worrying!
Letter following.'

That's not kind.

The Finest Dinner

On a lecture tour of America, I was flown from one town to another where I met local celebrities at gourmet dinners. At a small airport in the Midwest I was met as usual by a smiling hostess who chatted happily about her French cookery classes, the results of which I would sample at dinner that evening.

On arrival at her home she showed me to my room, glancing at me thoughtfully as she went out. Before long she returned carrying a tray with a bottle of bourbon and a plate of sandwiches on it.

'But if I eat these I won't have room for your dinner,' I protested.

'You're not coming to my French dinner,' she replied calmly. 'You're going to sleep, Rabbi. You need it.'

I nearly cried with gratitude after she closed the door behind her. I slept and didn't wake up till the next morning. It was the finest dinner I never tasted.

A Sermon I Had Never Expected

The finest sermon I never heard
was given after I missed a train.
Having time on my hands, I
wandered into a Quaker meeting
taking place near the station.
The chairman opened the
meeting with a reading, then,
just as the silence began, a man
shambled in from the street and
ranted on about how he had been
defrauded by the monarchy, the
government, the opposition.

After forty minutes the chairman closed the meeting and all present lined up and quietly thanked the man for his testimony. He grumbled and shuffled off down the street.

In the train I thanked God for the patient goodness of people. It was a sermon I had never expected and have never forgotten.

Presents From Poor People

A telephone call to a lonely person – cost, only 10p.

Offer to clean out someone's cooker – provided you know how to put it back together again!

Give up a grudge against someone!

Your time: 'I promise ... two hours of my time for any service the recipient requires, provided it's not illegal, dangerous or fattening.'

A present for yourself

A morning lie-in, listening to the radio with a cup of tea.

And one for God

Five minutes of your attention.

Wisdom for Twopence

I bought the sayings of Marcus Aurelius, the Roman Emperor, for twopence when I was a boy. They've been my life companions and I recommend them to you.

'Tell yourself today,' he advises, 'that you'll meet a fool, an envious person and an ungrateful one. Tell yourself too that they don't know any better.'

'Don't rely on outer chapels,' he warns. 'Construct one inside yourself that is always open.'

'If God exists, follow him. If he doesn't, stand in for him and be like God yourself.'

Perfect?

Unlike the modern English sense of the word, the old Hebrew word for 'perfect' has the sense of 'whole' or 'complete'. This is an important distinction because perfectionism can destroy our confidence. In this imperfect world we need confidence to pick ourselves up, learn and try again.

Many years ago I tried to be a perfect cook. But God showed me that a fallen soufflé is only a risen omelette. It all depends on how you look at it. He also pointed out when I burnt my gourmet dinner that he had created fish and chip shops for just that situation.

The Most Important Religious Question

My mother, who was not religious, asked me the most religious question of all:

'Lionel,' she said, 'will all that religion make you nicer?'

'I'm not sure,' I replied hesitantly. 'Religion can make you very nice or very nasty. I think it's made me nicer than I would have been without it.'

It's a test I apply to all religion.

Meditation

I went to a guru who tried to teach me to still my mind through meditation.

'Your mind,' he said, 'is a screen. A succession of shadows flickers across it. They are your feelings of anger, ambition, love and hatred.'

He then asked me two simple questions which I have pondered all my life: 'Where do these shadows come from? Who or what projects them onto the screen that is your mind?'

Painting

My friend Irene tried to teach me to paint. She looked at one of my wooden attempts. It was a failure.

'Pour turps over it,' she ordered, 'then wipe the picture with a rag so the colours run into each other. Then turn it upside down. Then look into the canvas as you would a fire, seeing the pictures revealed in it. The shapes and colours suggest so much. Why, there's a house! There's a person on a road! There's a cloud! Develop them and help them reveal themselves. Don't worry about failure. Many failures are a necessary preparation for success.'

Dutch Honesty

Just after the war I went on my first holiday abroad on my own. A Dutch family invited me to tea. I licked my lips when I saw a plate of cream cakes on the table, a treat I hadn't enjoyed for years because rationing was still in force in post-war England. 'Have one, Lionel,' they invited.

Having been brought up to be polite, English style, I replied

'No, I really couldn't.' They should then have responded, 'Oh, but you must!' and pressed me to take one. I would then have selected the biggest and creamiest.

Being Dutch they never did. The plate was passed down to the other end of the table and never returned. I learned a lesson in honesty I have never forgotten.

Hillel

Here is a saying from Hillel, who lived just before Jesus. It has stuck in my mind and I sing it to a catchy tune:

'If I am not for myself, who will be for me? But if I am only for myself, am I worth bothering about? And if I don't put this into practice now, then when?'

Supernatural

What is the supernatural?
Nothing spooky. It's like this:

To like people who like you is
natural. To like people who don't
like you is not just natural, it is
more than natural. It is super-
natural, super-duper-natural!

Visiting Rights

When your parents die there is much unfinished business. Instead of muttering prayers when you visit their burial place or memorial, sit down quietly on a bench. Speak to them and let them speak in you. They can, because anyone you have loved lives on within you if you allow them space in your mind.

Not Moses

Rabbi Zusya said:

*'In the world to come they
will not ask me why I was
not Moses, but why I was
not Zusya.'*

They will ask you, too, why you
were not yourself.

Heaven

For some rabbis heaven is a permanent lecture course you never have to interrupt for food, either eating it or getting rid of it. God himself is the teacher. For the Reverend Sidney Smith it was eating paté to the sound of trumpets. But the best description comes from Abélard, the medieval theologian. According to Abélard, heaven is the place where you get what you have always wanted and when you have got it, it proves to be all you hoped for.

The Last Judgment

There is endless speculation as to the Last Judgment and what it will be like. Hardly any is convincing. Once I asked my teacher what he thought.

'All that will happen,' he said, 'is that God will take us one by one to Him (or Her). He will sit you

on His knee and show you what
your life was really about. You
will see all the good you did, and
all the bad, without illusion.
That will be your heaven and
hell.'

Gossip

A student of mine was asked to give a sermon at a home for the elderly, noted for the wicked gossip that circulated amongst its residents. 'I'll have to admonish them,' he said bravely. 'It's my duty, whatever they may say about me.'

'How did it go?' I asked him later.

'There were no complaints at all,' he replied, astonished and upset. 'In fact, they liked it! Everyone there came up to me afterwards, congratulated me on giving a wonderful sermon and said they knew exactly who I was getting at!'

Accepting criticism of ourselves isn't easy!

Pray About What's Really in Your Mind

During a storm the cart carrying St Teresa and her nuns keeled over, depositing them in the mud. 'Pray for us, Mother', begged her nuns.

St Teresa then knelt in the mud and prayed as follows: 'Lord, since this is the way you treat your friends, it is no wonder you have so few of them.'

When you pray, tell God what is really in your mind!

Rose of Lima

St Rose of Lima said:

'Instead of talking about God, talk to Him.'

Great Minds Think Alike

Hillel, in the years before Jesus, taught:

Who is happy? Those who are content with what they have got.

Who is wise? Those who learn from others.

Who is mighty? Those who conquer their own passions.

True Listening

An Anglican priest taught me to comfort a dying friend with my hand, not my mouth. He said, 'There's no need to say anything. Just sit beside him and hold his hand, responding lightly to any slight increase in pressure. Your touch means more than words.

'Don't clutch his hand. Let his lie loosely in yours. Then, when he wants to depart and go forward on his journey, he knows he has your permission. Let his hand slip gently out of yours.

'Stay by him until he no longer needs you. Pray for him and for yourself, and leave quietly. That is true listening, attending to him without a word being said.'

Empty

Lao-tzu, which means 'Old Boy', lived in China more than 2,500 years ago. He wrote that sometimes what is not there is more important than what is. The importance of a window is the hole in the wall through which light can enter. The importance of a cup is the empty space contained by the porcelain, which can be filled.

Sometimes the most blessed words are those you did not say during an argument, and the greatest honours those you did not accept to avoid making others envious.

Ageing

Don't be frightened of ageing! When I was 27 and my hair was falling out, I decided to commit suicide when I reached 30. I'm glad I didn't. There are lots of nice things about being 70. You don't have to be successful, you're out of the rat race and you can be yourself. You can ride buses and if you want to live on tinned pilchards, rice pudding and sausages, why not? As my mother said before she died, 'Lionel, what you've done, you've done and the rest is gravy.'

I'm not quite sure what she meant but it sounds upbeat and sensible.

Mirror

The simplest words can be the most deadly.

Try not to say 'Who cares?' or 'Why me?'

Try not to shrug you shoulders and pass by.

Try not to say 'That's not fair!' like a little child.

Life is unfair. But that is why you were created – to make it fairer.

Mystic Advice

In the mystic books of Judaism it is written that 'At your judgment God will ask you why you didn't enjoy all the things that were permitted to you.' So give yourself treats. It's your religious duty! I make myself cinnamon toast and watch old films with happy endings.

Sabbath

You don't have to be Jewish to enjoy the Sabbath. Here's how you do it:

On Friday evening invite your family to Sabbath supper. In a big city your family are often your friends.

Light two candles and the table begins to feel holy.

Give small inexpensive presents to your guests as a token of affection. If you can't afford to, give them some jokes or compliments.

Let everyone bring a dish. Then you won't feel badly used and hate your guests.

Tell each other any helpful things that happened during the past week.

The Sabbath magic turns friends into family, and a bedsit into a home.

Investment

Whenever you do something generous for heaven's sake, heaven comes very close. You feel its inner glow. Invest some of yourself in heaven now!

Anger

The Bible warns us not to bear grudges against our neighbours. If yours has done something unneighbourly, talk about it, but don't bottle it up! You don't have to be aggressive, just ask why. Remember, bottled-up anger can give you a migraine and make you depressed. Don't carry such a weight around with you! And be aware that it's often what you hate most in your neighbour that you hate in yourself.

Religious Experience

You decide to meet God at a service, but he doesn't show up. Well, it takes two to tango.

Later you go to a party and while you are standing there with a glass in one hand and a canapé in the other, chatting away, something does happen. A part of you separates itself from the rest of you and, from somewhere near the ceiling, looks down on you and all the party with compassion.

Many people experience such out-of-body experiences. Don't dismiss them. It's not just your imagination.

Prayer

What does prayer give me?

Well it doesn't exempt me from life's problems, nor does it reveal the secrets of the universe.

This is my personal testimony. I am one of those people who faint or feels queasy at the sight of blood. So it is one of life's ironies that I have to visit hospitals as a minister. As I go through the doors I pray, 'Help!' It works! I get the strength to do my job and only feel nausea when I come out.

Prayer shows me what I have to do next in life and provides me with that little extra strength to do it.

Business

You need more inner strength than ever in business. Competition is sharper and failure less tolerated. Life is also lonelier. Much of the time you stare alone into a computer. There is no one to congratulate you on your successes or commiserate with you on your failures.

Go on a retreat to renew your inner resources. Retreats come in all flavours – Anglican, Catholic, Quaker, Jewish, Methodist, Buddhist and many others. There is bound to be one for you.

Home

My grandfather left a little corner of his parlour unplastered to remember that, although his house seemed solid, it wasn't his eternal home. It was more a temporary shelter, like a tent.

I concluded the same thing during the Second World War. The first thing we did in the morning after an air raid during the night was to see if our house was still standing.

One morning it wasn't. There was just a big black hole instead. My mother got hold of a barrow. We piled whatever was left into it and wheeled it to the lockup used for people who had been bombed out. I have never believed in the permanence of earthly homes since.

My real home is in another dimension. Knowing this has saved me much unnecessary pain.

Easter Egg

An elderly nun told me that as a child at Easter she had to search for a hard-boiled egg that was hidden in the garden and, when she found it, crack open the shell and eat it. The garden, of course, represented Gethsemane. The eggshell she cracked was the tomb of Jesus, the egg white His clothes and Jesus was the yolk, the meat inside.

You don't have to learn theology through your mind, you can also digest it and learn it through your taste buds. After all, we talk of the milk of human kindness and the odour of sanctity!

Grave

Many years ago as I was throwing a spadeful of earth into a grave, I fell in. It was probably my epilepsy, which I hadn't yet spotted. When they got me out, the other mourners said, 'You must have been thinking very profound thoughts down there, Rabbi.'

I answered uncomfortably, 'Ye-es, ye-es.'

Later my mother asked, 'What were you really thinking down there, Lionel?' And I confessed, 'I was thinking, "It must have been a pretty solid coffin. Thank God it was an expensive funeral!"'

My mother wasn't shocked. She just said, 'Always tell the truth, especially to yourself, and never, never put on the style.' And that was the best advice ever!

Night Duty

Your watch says 1.30 a.m., not p.m., and you can't sleep. The house is silent and you feel awfully alone.

Actually, you are not alone. You are in good company.

Think about the people of the night who are also awake, like you. Long-distance lorry drivers, nightclub hostesses, contemplative nuns keeping vigil, office cleaners, people desperately searching for partners in bars, nurses on duty, people waiting for prescriptions, people in pain, people in passion.

Don't just think about them, pray for them as well as yourself. Some of them, like the nuns and an evangelical lorry driver I know, are thinking and praying for you, so it's only fair.

Divorce

To be honest you don't need much God for nice occasions such as coming together and marrying. But you need a lot of God when you're parting or divorcing. That's when you feel loneliness and failure. There are no services to help you and not many people around to support you. But if you can rid yourself of bitterness and not deny the love that was once there and the affection that may still remain, then you have parted well.

Congratulate yourself even if nobody else does and may God bless you!

Chocolate

'Chocolate,' I thought, puzzled, 'used to taste so much more chocolatey when I was a kid.' As a kid I had to bless all food, including chocolate, and only then was I allowed to suck it. This increased my anticipation, which made the flavour more intense.

Now I gobble it when I'm nervous and wonder why it doesn't taste so chocolatey.

If you want your food to taste better, eat it slowly and say a blessing. That's as good as any gourmet recipe.

Rows

Having rows is human. Making
up is divine, in every sense.

A Pancake

Some good Taoist advice:

*Rule yourself or a country
as you would turn a
pancake – with care!*

Letter to a Child

Tidying out a drawer, I came upon
a faded photograph of the child I
once was long ago. I suddenly
wanted to write a letter to that
child, warning him of what life
would bring.

'Dear child', I wrote and set out
the advice that I had learnt so

painfully, that would have saved him so much grief and suffering.

Was it a foolish exercise? No, because the child we once were still lives on deep inside us, though not one cell of our bodies is any longer the same.

Old Quarrels

At a cocktail party a friend said, 'Let's go and talk to that couple over there!' I hesitated and he asked me why. I told him we'd quarrelled bitterly fourteen years before and had never spoken since. 'What was it about?' he asked, interested. What indeed!

I couldn't explain because I'd forgotten. So I went over and after
a few cautious minutes they were
charming.

Life is short, we are OAPs
together and all quarrels and
vendettas have their sell-by date.
This was long past it.

Be Prepared

If you want to die well, don't leave the preparations too late. When you are young and in good health, don't be afraid of meditating on death and reading about it. Then it will come as no surprise and you will not panic when the time comes. It might even be pleasant, like a holiday.

Life Beyond Life

When you die, time and space die with you so there is no 'after' life. But there is a beyond life and you can make yourself familiar with it and enjoy it even in this life.

Real Religion in the Real World

When I first caught religion I
tried very hard to shut out the
silly, secular world around me,
with its rows and rumpus, and
concentrate on eternity instead.
I wanted some special revelation
to fall from heaven and hit me –
bonk! – on the head in the high
street. My life would then be
bathed in blessings, obvious to
any discerning believer.

Well, it was fun while it lasted – though it didn't last long, because real holiness doesn't happen that way. The real knowledge of God came to me for example while I was cooking cabbage in the kitchen or riding a bad-tempered camel on a package holiday. Faith was funnier than I had expected, and to be honest, religion more real than I really wanted.

A Suburban Sanctuary

Mine is an ordinary semi in a suburb, but it is not a *machine à habiter*.

It is a sanctuary where friends become family, where sentimental rubbish is treated with reverence and where more prayers are said than in a synagogue.

Mysticism on the Move

Holidays expose the hidden workings of mind and soul because they are the point at which reality and fantasy meet. Travel takes me away from my built-in defences. Forlorn in foreign parts and unfamiliar hotels, holiness is the only home available. I have to match my outer journey with an inner one. I am more mystical on the move. Spiritually speaking, tourism turns me on.

Room Service

I am a worldly person, who has tried for years to be detached and other-worldly. I have moaned in monasteries and gone after gurus to get this experience or that which I am told is a mystical must. But I get nearest to it when I am perched in a private and impersonal pad on the fifteenth floor of a hotel block. I am insulated against the world and feel nowhere. It's a necessity as well as a pleasure to pray in such a place – and it's on the house!

The Basics of Belief

Apart from professional theologians who are paid to puzzle over definitions and dogmas, most people keep well away from them. Many turn instead to religious experience, which seems refreshing, simple and sensuous, but it is no substitute for the hard stuff.

The basics of belief have to be sorted out, and a cemetery is a gentle place to do it. Sitting on a bench, you can consider death, doom, sin, salvation – the lot. When you work out what they mean to you personally, they lose some of their strangeness and a lot of their terror. If you treat them with respect but without idolatry you begin to know where you stand – which makes life a lot less confusing in this world and the next.

The Hard Stuff

Belief in God is no guarantee against a disaster. When this message hits home, you either lose faith or get converted to it properly. Conversion doesn't mean changing religious brand names, just accepting the implications of what you've got. A teacher told me this tale from the Cabbala, the hidden heart of Judaism:

'Before God created the universe, He abandoned a part of Himself, to leave an emptiness in which we and the world could exist in freedom. In the emptiness are scattered sparks of His shattered divinity. It is our duty to redirect them back to God – to reassemble and to reunite Him, so to speak.'

God is not above disaster; He suffers in it. His sparks are in those who risk their lives to save others, and all who give generously of their time and money to help the victims.

A Brit Abroad

An engine driver I met in
America many years ago asked
me why I didn't stay over there. I
bit into a doughnut and puzzled
it out, for I found the people,
their cuisine and the landscape
quite lovely. I told him it was
because they lacked one freedom
that I couldn't do without.

I wanted the freedom to be a failure, or at any rate not to be a success, because that makes life very tense and worrying and I am anxiety prone enough as it is. In America the pressures were so much stronger and the competition so much tougher.

Competition had a funny effect on religion, too. It was as if everybody had changed roles.

The believers never stopped talking about fund-raising, nor the unbelievers about the state of their souls. Together they packed the pews or queued for the couches at their analysts. At home, in London, nobody was very interested in 'getting on', either in this world or the next.

What is Religion?

I stood outside a synagogue as the evening prayers ended. A nearly blind old man in tattered clothes pressed a shilling into my hand. I tried to give it back but he said, 'Everybody could use a shilling.'

He invited me to his attic room and made me lemon tea among his piles of papers, books and folios

(I later learnt that he was the last great mystic rabbi and Cabbalist in London.)

I asked him questions that I had never dared to ask my other teachers. 'What is religion?' I asked.

'The art of giving without strings,' he replied.

I still think about such an unexpected answer.

I Resolve ...

My favourites; I make them again
and again:

> I resolve not to spray paint
> on a door with a dog flap.
> My dog was black and the
> paint was puce.

> I resolve to remember that
> there is a little Nazi in me.

> I resolve to make marmalade
> without cheating and using

an orange jelly to help it
set.

I resolve to remember that
dog chocs are meant for my
dog, not me.

I shall try to remember that
I do not have to earn God's
love.

Poor Fish

Once a scavenger, always a scavenger, and I examine the debris after the party to see if I can make a mixed hors d'oeuvre. Well, there is a slice of salmon, lightly dusted with cigar ash, a truffle with a tooth mark and a pickled herring still wearing its head, but not much else.

I had expected something better,

so I retire to an armchair and count my blessings in the year just gone, the real ones, not the obvious ones. I think about the answer a Christian minister I know gave me when I asked him to explain the doctrine of the Fall.

'It means,' he said, 'accepting that you're an imperfect person in an imperfect world and acting accordingly.'

And that is what I did, for it suited my situation. I blew the ash off the salmon and added my tooth mark to the truffle. But I covered the herring head with a serviette because it didn't look so sanguine, poor fish!

A Communion Cup of Tea

I wandered into a strange church to say a prayer for a friend who had died. It seemed her sort of place, a church where she might have worshipped. I prayed for her, but I felt like an outsider and decided to hurry away as soon as I decently could.

As I was about to go I was waylaid in the church hall by a friendly woman who put a cup of tea in one of my hands and a big slice of cake in the other. It dawned on me that another sort of service was taking place in the church hall. This time it was the ladies who ministered to me with their tea and cakes, and because they did so with a good heart, it was a kind of communion, though cosy and with lots more calories. The minister came up too, shook my hand and refreshed my cup. This time he didn't preach about kindness, he just did me a kindness – it was the best sermon of all. I suddenly saw everyone in the hall as God meant me to see them.

The Real Answer

A rabbi said to God, 'I don't want Your heaven and I'm not scared of Your hell. I only want You.'

That's the real answer, though I'm not religious enough yet to cope with it.

Foaming Begonia

It is difficult to know what to do with the manna of scraps, sachets and bath salts that descend on us at Chanuka and Christmas time. I look over my loot, wondering what to make of the bottle of Foaming Burmese Begonia bath essence.

If presents can only be objects, it becomes very difficult to know what to give the Almighty at Christmas. What do you give to a Being who has everything?

I think the only present you can give God is your attention. Just a moment of it in the kitchen if that's all you have, freely snatched from the turkey and transferred to God, may be all He wants and very precious in His sight.

Far better than all the Foaming Burmese Begonia of which He must have bottles and bottles, thank you, since He created the lot!

Good Taste

A religious lesson by mouth, not
in your ear:

> Mash a hard-boiled egg
> (free range) in a small bowl
> of salt water. The salt water
> represents the tears and the
> egg the new life that
> springs from them.

It's a Passover dish, and a tasty
one.

A Rucksack of Memories

Hope was in short supply in 1939. A Nazi invasion was expected daily and the great evacuation began. I was uprooted from the snug, warm, Slav-Jewish world I knew and evacuated into another, gentile, world.

One grey morning during that grey time I wandered into a

church. It was Christmas time and I got into conversation with an elderly lady who tried to explain the Christmas story. When I told her I was a Jew she put away the little book about Jesus she may have intended to give me, thought for a moment and asked me to wait. She returned with a white sugar mouse that glittered. She gave it to me and said she would pray for the Jews in Germany who had nothing but prayer to help them.

From that point on something began to glow in my greyness. I had made contact with kindness, though it wore a different dress and spoke in strange symbols. There was goodness outside my ghetto as well as inside, and this was a great discovery.

Success and Failure

I was considered a bright child, and highly commended for my encyclopaedic knowledge of Adam Smith and my astonishing knack with Aramaic verbs. But my successes have never got me very far. No one has ever asked me about either Adam Smith or Aramaic verbs. What people like to hear about are my weaknesses: my clumsiness, how I fell into a grave and off a pulpit, and the terrible faux pas I make.

Late in life the penny has dropped. We can never know our successes and failures. Only God can distinguish which is which. Some He works through and they bring blessing. Some remain as arid and unfulfilled as certificates won at school for subjects we scarcely remember.

Financial Blues

I turned on the radio one morning to hear there had been a fall on the stock market. There go my savings and my security, I thought!

Although the fall was only a financial hiccup, it made a lot of people like me a bit sick with self-pity. But you don't have to lose your soul with your savings.

The wise men said that the more you lose, the more you should give to charity. Then you will realise that there is always someone worse off than you, and though this won't make you richer, it will make you *feel* richer.

Sense and Nonsense

We human beings are a little higher than the animals and a little lower than the angels.

We are animals because usually only what we can sense, what we can touch, see, hear or smell, seems real to us.

We are angels because we were the first animals to know that sometimes what is beyond or outside our senses can also be real – like God, conscience or spirit.

We are in-between creatures, who have begun to realise that what is not sense is not non-sense. But it is a struggle!

Give God a Break

For God's sake, don't be too dismal in your prayers! Why do you have to list all your mistakes? You've had some successes too. After all, you've survived – you're still here, if only just. Why depress God as well? He has enough to contend with, without you being damp and droopy too.

The Ball

On my way back from work, my mind is full of anger, annoyance and self-pity – the debris of my working day.

I roll them into a ball in my mind and mentally throw it up to heaven, saying, 'Catch!' Which I think God must do, because I don't usually worry what went wrong anymore.

Journeys in Faith

I was blown into other religions because of the Blitz and, though bewildered, found I enjoyed them. Perhaps it was because of the war, but there was more welcome than I expected. Lots of people like to boast that their own religion remains unaffected by such contact.

Mine wasn't, and I'm glad of it. I was able to learn from a universe that was bigger and richer beyond all belief than my own parish piety.

Do It Yourself

'Why this division in the nature of things,

This endless struggle between truth and truth?'

So wrote Boethius 1,500 years ago. The choice between truth

and truth tears our religion apart. Like many who have rejected fundamentalism or guruism, I have had to put together my piety piece by piece. The result may seem poor, but it is honest, and tougher than you might credit, for it is tried and tested in my life.

A Sympathetic Ear

When I first became a rabbi I thought I would be needed most for talking and sermons and such. But the most valuable thing I've had to learn is how to listen.

Sympathetic listening is a vocation for anyone who can spare a little time in a busy life and make a sacrifice of his or her impatience and boredom in the service of God. You can listen anywhere. Churches and synagogues are not necessary. An office does just as well. So does a pub, or a park bench.

Humdrum Lives

My greatest problem is so humdrum and small it might seem silly. Like lots of ordinary people, I suffer from stress, worry and mild depression as I face the day. On bad days I can't draw the curtains and the telephone makes me tremble.

It took me a long time to realise that redemption was hidden in little things – like boots, brushes and polish. As the leather begins to glow, some hope begins to glow in me.

I can't cope with serious deeds, but the little kindnesses I give and receive bring back my courage, and make all the difference in a depression.

Brightening Up

When I'm down, I don't bellow
out brave blessings. I squeak out
'All Things Bright and Beautiful'
instead, in a shaky voice, and it
works – the world seems a bit
brighter.

God Only Knows

Only God can know what is big and small in a human life, what is heroic or humdrum, what unnoticed bravery is required by ordinary people trying to do ordinary things in their ordinary lives.

Pretending

As a child I did a lot of pretending. Like pretending I lived in a house with two bow windows. (I was mortified when school friends called by and counted them.)

Later on, I pretended I was only embarking on rabbinical training for the most high-minded motives. They were true as far as they went, but there were other motives I didn't admit to my examiners or myself. Like:

> What else could I do with a second-class Arts degree?

> Becoming a rabbi would give me social status.

> Because I liked the sound of my own voice.

But when I finally admitted them to God and myself, I didn't feel like a fraud any more, and it was right to have become a rabbi.

No Spiritual Snob

If you ever find that you're reduced to gabbling your prayers, give your mind a rest and pray with your body instead.

Dance and sing in the privacy of your bedroom or bathroom, and feel God's joy flow into you. Bounce on your bed if you wish, or even pretend to be your pet!

God created your body – don't be a spiritual snob about it!

Seeking Out the Truth

Lots of people want to take a trip to heaven – many get taken for a ride.

Some seek out holy men in the Himalayas. Some practise austerities, and some smoke their way to the sublime. Some discover deep contemplation; some end up in cloud-cuckoo-land, and some in asylums. Are their journeys really necessary?

We all have to journey through the world outside us to discover the truths we already possess inside us.

Angels

Angels are beings who bring us messages from heaven. They take the form of people or animals.

Mine wore shawls, not haloes, and black shoes with slits for their bunions, not sandals. They didn't fly but waddled.

They used to take me out with them at night when I was a child. They put packets of food or pennies into the letterboxes of houses where no one had work. They did this at night so that giver and receiver need never recognise each other. That is how angels give.

Seeing a Soul

To see a soul, wander into an art gallery or museum, and sit in front of a Rembrandt portrait. Not a portrait of a young face, but of an old one – perhaps one of his later self-portraits.

The outer flesh has worn thin; it is wrinkled, blotched and pale.

But this makes the inner light in that face seem even stronger and brighter.

Many artists paint the flesh. Rembrandt painted the emerging soul that survives it. See for yourself!

Parties

When you give a party, don't
force everyone to be cheerful and
sparkle. You don't know what's
going on in their lives or minds.
If someone's moody, let them sit
on their own. Make sure there's
some beer and sandwiches close
by and give them the freedom to
get on with it. That's real
kindness.